Introd

Don't settle on your sex life...

Remember that time when you and your partner were just starting to have sex together? Do you remember the passion? The lust? Do you often look at fresh couples and secretly feel a little jealous in their passion for each other?

Sex is one of the main pleasures life has to offer. At the end of the day, everything we do in life is simply to satisfy our primal instincts – Food, shelter, and sex.

While we strive to enjoy better meals whenever we can and strive to improve our shelters (Improving our homes, moving to bigger houses), we often neglect one of our biggest drives in life - sex. And this might become a subconscious source of suffering and unhappiness.

In this book, you're going to experience sex as you've never experienced before. You're going to get multiple orgasms, mind-blowing sex positions, and stretch your comfort zone.

This book will strengthen your relationship, and rekindle your passion for each other. Here is how:

1

You're about to face 100 sex challenges, quests, and games. All of them must be completed.

At the end of this book, you'll have a checklist with the names of the challenges. Whenever you finish a challenge, tick the box. You finish when all of the 100 boxes are ticked.

Rules for The Sex Bucket List

Rule #1: Do not skip things you've already done – if you face a challenge that you had the chance to experiment, do not tick the box. You must do it again.

Rule #2: Like a Virgin – approach each challenge as if it were the first time you're having sex (or doing the task). Keep an open mind and approach the challenges with curiosity and excitement.

Rule #3: Use markers – When you finish with a challenge, mark it. I recommend using markers in 3 colors: red, green and blue.

Red represents challenges you didn't enjoy very much.

Green represents challenges you liked and would love to try again.

Blue represents challenges that you're not so sure about but would like to try again.

Rule #4: Take Turns – The challenge isn't over until both of you experienced both sides of it. Yes, that includes anal challenges.

Ready? Steady? Go!

The Sex Bucket List

<u>Challenge #1:</u>
<u>Follow the Porn</u>

Watch a porn video with your partner, doing the exact same position as it appears on the porn video. Do not choose a boring video. Choose a porn video where there a lot of different positions that you haven't tried.

<u>Challenge #2: Hot tub fun</u>

Get inside a hot tub with a bottle of Champaign and start talking. When you feel a little tipsy, you can start kissing each other and raise the heat until you're having sex. If you don't have a hot tub in your home, book a romantic spa treatment for both of you and make sure they have a hot tub in the room. Don't be cheap – it's worth every penny.

Challenge #3: Mirror Masturbation

Masturbate while your partner is masturbating herself/himself as well. Both must be naked and sitting across from each other, either on the opposite sides of the bed or in 2 chairs/sofas/etc.

Challenge #4: Sweet 16

Have a dry humping for 20 minutes, without removing your clothes. Make out, kiss necks, grab hair, anything you want – but don't take your clothes off. When things get hotter, you can stay in your underwear. However, make sure that you do this for at least 20 minutes before you start having sex.

Challenge #5: Naughty Lunch Break

At lunch break, meet your partner and have sex in the middle of the day. You can have sex in your car, in a secret place that you know, or even rent a room at a close-by hotel. When you finish, get back to work as if nothing happened.

Challenge #6: Foot Fetish

For 10 minutes, lick your partner's feet. You can use a water-based edible lube to make this even sexier.

Challenge #7:
Sloppy Blowjob

Give your partner the sloppiest blowjob you can ever give. Be messy. Be dirty. Let his cum rub all over your face and mouth. To add a cherry to the cream, let him cum in your mouth.

*Note – Some women have difficulty to enjoy the sperm of the man. If that is the case, ask your man to avoid for 2 days:

Nicotine

Junk food

Coffee

Onion & Garlic

And ask him to eat a lot of pineapple and vegetables.

Remember that you're supposed to get outside of your comfort zone. Even if you don't like the taste of it, take this sacrifice and let your man enjoy this challenge.

Challenge #8: Sex Shopping

Go to a sex shop and buy a toy for your girl. Buy something that she'd like to try in bed. Don't be shy – ask the owner for help to find something recommended that will make your woman enjoy.

Challenge #9: Phone Sex

Call your partner when you're separated for the night. Do not use the camera. Start touching yourself while speaking with your partner. Tell your partner what you'd like to do him right now, and he should respond with what he'd like to do you.

Challenge #10: You're under arrest

Use handcuffs, or an old piece of clothes to tie your partner's hands behind their back. Have sex without letting your partner release their hands. Next time – switch turns.

Challenge #11: Ice Ice Baby

Ice can be an amazing upgrade to your sex life. Bring a pack of ice cubes to the bedroom. Start with eating the ice and then give oral sex to each other. Play with the ice cubes on your partner's neck, chest, nipples, and gently over their genitals. You can get as creative as you'd like.

Challenge #12: Skype Sex

While separated, call your partner using FaceTime/skype. Start touching yourself while watching your partner enjoying the show as well. You can add some sex noise if you'd like to spice things up.

Challenge #12: Candles Atmosphere

Décor your bedroom with candles. Use candles with warm, tasty scents. The atmosphere will put both of you in a romantic mood that will make your sex much more interesting.

Challenge #13: Candles Massage

Use skin-safe candles and melt them down on your partner. The temperature and sense of hot wax on the skin will be very sexy.

Challenge #15: Pool Sex

If you've never tried to have sex in a pool, you're missing out a lot of fun.

If you have a pool in your house that's easy – just make sure that nobody's watching and get inside the pool ready for action. You can add some chairs, floaters and other equipment to help you function in the water.

If you don't have a pool, go on AirBNB and spoil yourself for the weekend. Rent a house with a pool only for the weekend and explore yourself in the water.

Challenge #16: Sex on the Beach

Bring a big towel that both of you can lay on. Go to a quiet beach and watch the sunset with a bottle of wine. Once the sun is down, start kissing each other towards having sex. If you see no one around, you can have sex in the sunset to add a romantic atmosphere.

Challenge #17: Loud as you can

Have sex and try to be as loud as you possibly can. Scream, Thrust, yell, curse, whatever it is that will help you to make this sex way louder than usual.

Challenge #18:
Mirrors Everywhere

Place mirrors around your bed in a way that no matter where you look, you can see each other

Challenge #19: Sex Vipassana

This one is a little more challenging than the others.

At the beginning of the weekend, turn off your phones, internet, TV, and any other device that might steal your attention. This weekend you will focus only on having sex with each other, without any other stimulations.

Challenge #20: Sex Tape

Place your phone on a chest or a table in your bedroom, such that it will be able to record you having sex. Record yourself having sex in various positions. Enjoy when you watch it later.

Challenge #21: Laundry Machine Sex

Turn on your laundry machine and let the girl sit on it. Have sex while the machine works, vibrating and shaking your girl in every way possible.

Challenge #22: Handjob While Driving

Give your man a handjob while he is driving. Try to make him cum. If your husband is a bad driver, you can do this in a traffic jam.

Challenge #23: Nothing but heels

Wear high heels when your man gets back home. Make sure your clothes can be easily removed without removing your heels. Have sex with your man without removing the heels from your feet.

Challenge #24: High socks

Have sex while wearing nothing but high socks

Challenge #25: Go to a strip club together

Sharing an activity like going to a strip club together can be a good way to strengthen trust in the relationship, and hence, improving your sex life.

Go to a strip club as a couple. Drink, have a lap-dance, enjoy the show! When you get back home, you can have a really sexy time.

Challenge #26: Silent Sex

Have sex while trying to be as silent as possible. No hard thrusts, no screams, no talking. In this challenge, you're trying to keep it low-key.

Challenge #27: Camping sex

Go to camping together. Relax and enjoy nature. Have sex a tent or outside, wherever you prefer.

Challenge #28: Fireplace sex

In a cold winter evening, turn on your fireplace and place a rug next to it. Have sex while the fireplace is burning next to you. If you don't have a fireplace or an attractive living room, you can rent a house with a fireplace from Airbnb.

Challenge #29: Good Morning Honey

Surprise your partner with oral sex as a way to wake him/her up in the morning

Challenge #30: Club Toilet Sex

Go to a nightclub together, have a few drinks, and go to the toilets together to have sex. If you know a place where the toilets are clean and nice that would be more recommended.

Challenge #31: Erotic Massage

Give your partner a massage while she/he is fully naked. Use hot almonds oil to rub her skin. Make sure that you rub all of the body, including the interesting places.

Challenge #32: Oiled Up

You and your partner will rub yourselves with oil and have sex with oily, shiny skins.

Challenge #33: Whipped Cream Sex

Add whipped cream can to the bedroom. Put it on your partner's body and eat it with passion. Have fun with it and get as creative as you can.

Challenge #34:
Anal sex

Whether you do it usually or not, anal sex is a great way to stretch your comfort zone (both for men and women). If you're new to anal sex, it's important to use lube. Start with only a finger or two to warm up. Then, you can continue to "bigger instruments".

Challenge #35: Violent Sex

Have violent sex together. Spank hard, slap on the face, grab the ass as hard as you can, and be dominant in the bedroom.

Challenge #36:
Free Use

While your partner is busy with another task (on the phone, reading, watch TV), take her clothes off and start having sex while she keeps doing her task.

Challenge #37: Lingerie Shopping

This challenge is sex free but it will spice things up sexually. Go together to a lingerie shop. Let your woman run the show and wear sexy outfits. Choose the outfit that is the sexiest in your opinion. Let your woman surprise you by wearing that in an unexpected time.

Challenge #38: Childhood Bedroom

As a teenager, you probably fantasized about sex. A lot. Go to your childhood/teenage room and have sex with your partner there.

Challenge #39: 20-minutes of kissing

For 20 minutes, do nothing but kissing passionately.

Challenge #40: Rewind a Date

Go to a place where you had a date. After you finish with your date, have sex in the car, or drive home for a successful date ending.

*It doesn't have to be your first date – you can choose any date that was fun for both of you.

Challenge #41: Cinema Sex

In a day where the cinema isn't that busy, sit in a dark place and have sex. If that's too much for you, you can just finger/blow/give a handjob.

Challenge #42: Sex Restriction

For 2 weeks, avoid having ANY sexual playtime. Both of you must be aware of the restriction period.

While this may sound counterproductive, restricting sex can increase your passion and attraction to each other – and the sex will be much more fun afterward.

Challenge #43: Sexting

Exchange at least 20 pictures with each other. Take your clothes off, wear sexy underwear, picture yourself in sexy positions on the bed, do whatever you'd like to make this challenge as sexy as you can.

Challenge #44: Text Sex

When you're apart, have text sex. Stat with explaining how you want to kiss…and then touch…and increase the temperature as your partner is seducing you with texts.

Challenge #45: Surprise!

Welcome your partner when he/she gets back home while being totally naked.

Challenge #46: Read Erotica

When you're in bed together, pull up a nice erotica book and read together. This can increase your sexual attraction and you may find in common a lot of things that you find hot

Challenge #47: Striptease

Give your partner a special striptease show. If you aren't sure how to do it, simply watch some YouTube videos and learn. It doesn't have to be perfect – it's the intention that counts.

Challenge #48: Bar Pick Up

Let your partner go to a bar and have a drink alone. Next, come in, and try to pick up your girl and take her home with you. Be careful; She's not easy to get…

Challenge #49: Never have I ever

Play never have I ever. Start with general questions, and then narrow down to sexual questions.

Challenge #50: Experiment Viagra

This challenge should be advised with a doctor before you do it.

Viagra can help you perform like a rockstar in bed and give your women an unforgettable night. Remember – you should advise a doctor before taking this challenge.

Challenge #51: Remote Controlled Vibrator

Purchase a remote controlled vibrator. Before you go out with your partner, ask her to put it in her panties. Play with the remote control in restaurants, in traffic jams, it's your choice!

Challenge #52: Lifeguard Stand

In the night when everybody leaves, sneak into the lifeguard's stand at the beach and have sex over there.

Challenge #53: Drive-thru

Make your partner cum while you're waiting in the line of a drive-thru.

Challenge #54: Sex Club

Go to a sex club together. Make sure to respect the dress code. If you're too embarrassed, go to a club that allows masks.

Challenge #55: Sex Dice

Purchase a pair of sex dice and play with them

Challenge #56: Under stars

In a place where you can see the stars clearly (Rooftop, nature, beach), have sex. When you finish, you can cuddle together and have a deep talk while the stars shine above you.

Challenge #57:
Totally new haircut

Surprise your partner and get a haircut that you've never done before. You can dye your hair, cut it, change it looks, whatever you'd like!

Challenge #58: Naked Twister

Play Twister together - totally naked.

Challenge #59: Sex in a barn

Find a barn (or again, rent it on Airbnb), and have sex there. Make sure you bring a blanket so you won't get too dirty.

Challenge #60:
Igloo Hotel Sex

Get a room in an Igloo hotel and have sex in this unique environment.

Challenge #61: Sex Under a Rock

Go hiking together and find a massive stone that will hide you both while you have sex in the open air.

Challenge #62: Trampoline Sex

Have sex on a trampoline

Challenge #63:
Hammock Sex

Have sex on a hammock

Challenge #64: Strip Poker

Play strip poker together

Challenge #65: Pay-for-Sex Roleplay

Negotiate with your partner for sex. Start with a negotiation about a handjob. As your partner provides you with a handjob, negotiate about a blowjob. Then – negotiate for sex. And if you are really in the mood, negotiate for kinky things.

Here's the catch, though – you actually must pay what you offer!

Challenge #66: Special Piercing

Get a piercing together. Choose a place on the body that will turn you on.

<u>Challenge #67:</u>
<u>Nipples Only</u>

For 20 minutes, do
nothing but playing
with your partner's
nipples.

Challenge #68: Rip her clothes

When things get hotter in bed, literally rip your partner's clothes. The includes the panties. Make sure that your partner is wearing cheap clothes that she doesn't mind to rip.

<u>Challenge #69:</u>
<u>69</u>

Make each other cum
from doing the 69
position

Challenge #70: No one can hear you

Use tape to tape your partner's mouth and have sex that will make her want to scream as hard as she can.

Challenge #71: Yoga/Gym outfit

Yoga and gym outfits can be extremely sexy. Before your partner leaves the house for her yoga class or workout, stop her and have sex.

Challenge #72: Have sex on a Ferris wheel

Who doesn't like amusement parks? Take a ride on a Ferris wheel (preferably when it's dark outside), and have sex. If that's too extreme for you, you can simply touch each other and give handjob/blowjob/fing er.

Challenge #73:
Special Sex Motel

Old, dusty motels belong to the previous century. Today, there are modern sex motels, with special rooms and different themes. Simply search on google "sex motel" and book a room for both of you.

Challenge #74: Party at Home

Put some music, get some drinks, and have a private party at home. As the party progresses, get naked, start kissing, and have mind-blowing sex.

Challenge #75: Glory hole sex

Take a large piece of cardboard and glue it to one of your room entrances. Cut a hole so the male can put his dick inside. Have sex and enjoy!

Challenge #76: Dressing Room

While shopping, go to a quiet clothing shop and have sex in a dressing room

Challenge #77: Threesome

This may be a hard challenge for most of the couples to accept – but if you're looking for a way to spice up your sex life, a threesome can actually shake things up. Simply go on tinder and search for another partner. You can be discreet and use fake names.

Challenge #78: Join the Mile-high Club

Have sex in an airplane's bathroom.

If you're too afraid to get in trouble with legal issues, there are actually specific charter flights for people who want to have sex up in the skies. Run a simple search on google "Charter Flights for Sex".

Challenge #79: Sauna Sex

Have sex in a hot sauna.

Challenge #80: Love notes

This challenge is less about sex and more about romance, which can bond you better and spike attraction. Simply leave love notes for your partner, telling them how much you appreciate, love, respect and happy to be in a relationship with.

Challenge #81: Use Earbuds

Having sex while restricting specific senses can make the experience appear completely new and very exciting. In this challenge, simply have sex while wearing earbuds.

Challenge #82: Blowjob under table

When your partner is sitting at his desk, simply crawl down, take his pants off, and give him a nice blowjob.

Challenge #83: Middle Ages Torture

Lay your partner on their back, tying up their hands and legs to the 4 corners of the bed. Take an eye-patch or a dark piece of clothes and cover their eyes. Do whatever you want with them until you cum. Next time, switch turns.

Challenge #84: Blind Sex

Take an eye patch or a dark shirt and tie around your partner's eyes. Have sex while your partner is blind. Next time – Switch turns.

Challenge #85: Edible panties

Buy edible panties and use them in bed.

Challenge #86: Sex on a boat

Rent a boat and have sex in a calm, quiet lake.

Challenge #87: Pitch Black

Have sex in a completely dark room. You can use black tape to tape your window, door, and every place where light can get in.

Challenge #88:
Quickie in a skirt

While your partner is wearing a skirt, bent her over for quick sex.

Challenge #89:
Feather ticklers

Use feather ticklers in bed. This challenge is best done when your partner is tied up.

Challenge #90: Swing Sex

Have sex on a swing.

Challenge #91: Balcony Sex

Have sex on a balcony.

Challenge #92: The Naked Chef

Cook and eat a meal together, completely naked.

Challenge #93: "Miracle Fruit Sex"

Have you heard about Miracle berry?

It is a special berry that changes your taste buds and makes you taste completely new flavors.

Order a miracle berry online and eat it together. Then, have sex, and focus on oral sex particularly.

Challenge #94: Download an app

The internet doesn't belong only to singles. Download those couple's apps: Happy Couple, Simply Us, Between, You & Me.

Challenge #95: Swingers Party

Go to a swinger's party. If that is not your thing, you can just watch.

Challenge #96: The Quiet Game

Spend a whole day without speaking with each other – no phone calls, no texts, no talks. Simply have sex through feeling the energy of each other.

Challenge #97:
Exercise Ball

Have sex using an exercise ball. Get as creative as you can. If you can't find any ideas, simply google: "Exercise Ball Sex".

Challenge #98: Tantric Sex

Take a course (or read a book) about Tantric sex, and apply.

Challenge #99: Candy Oral Sex

Give oral sex to your partner while having candy in your mouth.

Challenge #100: The Most Important Challenge

Commit to evolve sexually, romantically and emotionally forever. This is the hardest challenge – but it contains the biggest reward – a true, deep relationship.

Checklist

- O Challenge #1: Follow the Porn
- O Challenge #2: Hot tub fun
- O Challenge #3: Mirror Masturbation
- O Challenge #4: Sweet 16
- O Challenge #5: Naught Lunch Break
- O Challenge #6: Foot Fetish
- O Challenge #7: Sloppy Blowjob
- O Challenge #8: Sex Shopping
- O Challenge #9: Phone Sex
- O Challenge #10: You're under arrest
- O Challenge #11: Ice Ice Baby
- O Challenge #12: Skype Sex
- O Challenge #13: Candles Atmosphere
- O Challenge #14: Candles Massage
- O Challenge #15: Pool Sex
- O Challenge #16: Sex on the Beach
- O Challenge #17: Loud as you can
- O Challenge #18: Mirrors Everywhere

O Challenge #19: Sex Vipassana

O Challenge #20: Sex Tape

O Challenge #21: Laundry Machine Sex

O Challenge #22: Handjob While Driving

O Challenge #23: Nothing but heels

O Challenge #24: High socks

O Challenge #25: Go to a strip club together

O Challenge #26: Silent Sex

O Challenge #27: Camping sex

O Challenge #28: Fireplace sex

O Challenge #29: Good Morning Honey

O Challenge #30: Club Toilet Sex

O Challenge #31: Erotic Massage

O Challenge #32: Oiled Up

O Challenge #33: Whipped Cream Sex

O Challenge #34: Anal sex

O Challenge #35: Violent Sex

O Challenge #36: Free Use

O Challenge #37: Lingerie Shopping

- O Challenge #59: Sex in a barn
- O Challenge #60: Igloo Hotel Sex
- O Challenge #61: Sex Under a Rock
- O Challenge #62: Trampoline Sex
- O Challenge #63: Hammock Sex
- O Challenge #64: Strip Poker
- O Challenge #65: Pay-for-Sex Roleplay
- O Challenge #66: Special Piercing
- O Challenge #67: Nipples Only
- O Challenge #68: Rip her clothes
- O Challenge #69: 69
- O Challenge #70: No one can hear you
- O Challenge #71: Yoga/Gym outfit
- O Challenge #72: Have sex on a Ferris wheel
- O Challenge #73: Special Sex Motel
- O Challenge #74: Party at Home
- O Challenge #75: Glory hole sex
- O Challenge #76: Dressing Room

- O Challenge #77: Threesome
- O Challenge #78: Join the Mile-high Club
- O Challenge #79: Sauna Sex
- O Challenge #80: Love notes
- O Challenge #81: Use Earbuds
- O Challenge #82: Blowjob under table
- O Challenge #83: Middle Ages Torture
- O Challenge #84: Blind Sex
- O Challenge #85: Edible panties
- O Challenge #86: Sex on a boat
- O Challenge #87: Pitch Black
- O Challenge #88: Quickie in a skirt
- O Challenge #89: Feather ticklers
- O Challenge #90: Swing Sex
- O Challenge #91: Balcony Sex
- O Challenge #92: The Naked Chef
- O Challenge #93: "Miracle Fruit Sex"
- O Challenge #94: Download an app
- O Challenge #95: Swingers Party

Final Words

I hope you found at least 1 challenge that made you laugh, smile and strengthen your relationship.

If this book helped you, even just a little bit, I would really appreciate if you could leave a 5-star review on Amazon.

I read the reviews personally.

Further reading

If you enjoyed "The Sex Bucket List" by Sandra Simons, check out the book:

"Sex Positions"

Printed in Great Britain
by Amazon